Patterns in the
PARK

by J. Clark Sawyer

Consultant: Kimberly Brenneman, PhD
National Institute for Early Education Research, Rutgers University
New Brunswick, New Jersey

BEARPORT
PUBLISHING

New York, New York

Credits

Cover, © cooperr/Shutterstock; TOC, © Fedor Selivanov/Shutterstock; 4, © Martin Beddall/Alamy; 4–5, © Kent Kobersteen/National Geographic Society/Corbis; 6, © MkStock/Alamy; 6–7, © Karel Gallas/Shutterstock; 8–9, © Vivek Nigam/Thinkstock; 10–11, © Ocean/Corbis; 12–13, © Andrei Nekrassov/Alamy; 14–15, © YOSHIHIRO TAKADA/amanaimages/Corbis; 16, © Baloncici/Thinkstock; 17, © Erin Patrice O'Brien; 18–19, © Dasha Petrenko/Shutterstock; 20–21, © Frank Lukasseck/Corbis; 22, © Rodrigo Alvarez-Icaza/Getty Images; 23, © Teresa Kasprzycka/Dreamstime.com; 24–25, © Hellen Sergeyeva/Thinkstock; 26–27, © David Boag/Alamy; 28–29, © val lawless/Shutterstock; 30A, © Suzanne L. & Joseph T. Collins; 30B, © Carolyn Jenkins/ Alamy; 30C, © Alan Schein Photography/Corbis; 30D, © Darko Zeljkovic/Shutterstock; 31TL, © cooperr/Shutterstock; 31TM, © Fotog/Tetra Images/Corbis; 31TR, © Stephen J. Krasemann; 31BL, © javarman/Shutterstock; 31BR, © JoeFotoSS/Shutterstock.

Publisher: Kenn Goin
Editor: Jessica Rudolph
Creative Director: Spencer Brinker
Design: Debrah Kaiser
Photo Researcher: We Research Pictures, LLC

Library of Congress Cataloging-in-Publication Data

Clark Sawyer, J., author.
  Patterns in the park / by J. Clark Sawyer.
      pages cm.—(Seeing patterns all around)
  Includes bibliographical references and index.
  ISBN-13: 978-1-62724-339-1 (library binding)
  ISBN-10: 1-62724-339-9 (library binding)
  1. Pattern perception—Juvenile literature. 2. Shapes—Juvenile literature. 3. Parks—Juvenile literature. I. Title.
  BF294.C532 2015
  516.15—dc23
                              2014017381

For more information, write to Bearport Publishing Company, Inc., 45 West 21st Street, Suite 3B, New York, New York 10010. Printed in the United States of America.

10 9 8 7 6 5 4 3 2 1

Contents

Finding Patterns in the Park

Patterns can be shapes, colors, or sizes that repeat.

You can see patterns all around a park.

A row of bars makes a pattern of straight lines.

4

5

One duck in a pond does not make a pattern.

It does not repeat.

However, a row of
ducks makes a pattern.

A row of swings makes a pattern.

Short, long.

8

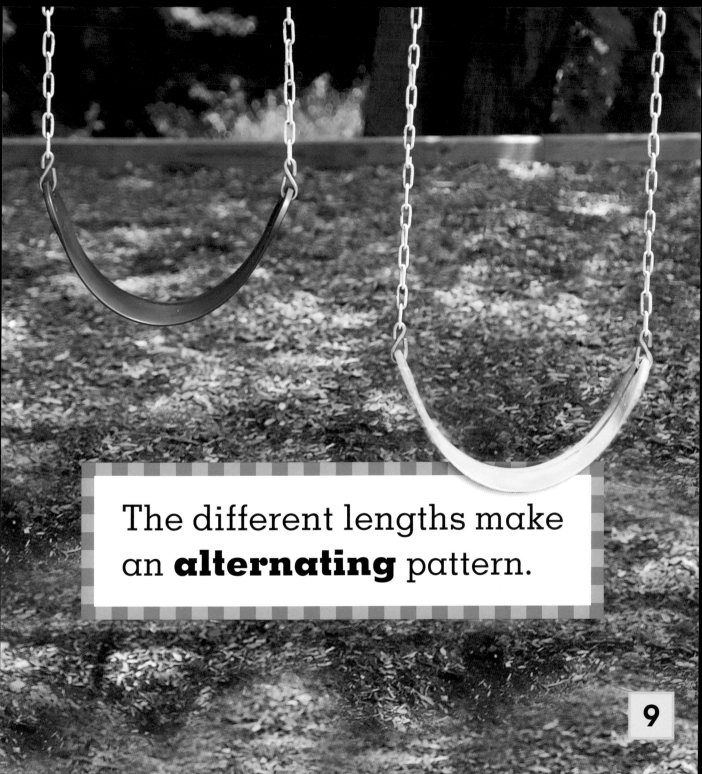

The different lengths make an **alternating** pattern.

Children on a merry-go-round make an alternating pattern, too.

Girl, boy.

The pattern repeats.

Lines on chairs make a striped pattern.

Green, white.

The colors repeat.

13

14

Rows of flowers
make a pattern.

Red, yellow.

The pattern repeats.

15

A table for playing games has alternating black and white squares.

This is called a **checkerboard** pattern.

Grass can have a checkerboard pattern, too.

White circles on a pink umbrella make a pattern of dots.

They are called polka dots.

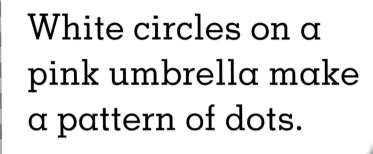

19

A **fawn** in a park looks for grass to eat.

Its white spots are different shapes and sizes.

They make an **irregular pattern**.

21

A climbing pole goes around and around in circles.

It makes a **spiral** pattern.

23

Some patterns have more than one shape.

24

Triangles and squares make up the pattern on this bridge.

A ground squirrel's fur has a pattern.

White stripe, brown stripe with white spots.

The pattern goes on.

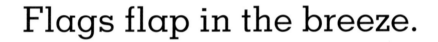

Flags flap in the breeze.

What patterns do you see on these flags?

Look all around to find patterns in a park!

Explore More:
Which Pattern?

Look at the pictures. Each one shows a kind of pattern that can be found in a park. Match each pattern with the correct picture.

1. polka-dot pattern

3. checkerboard pattern

2. irregular pattern

4. striped pattern

Answers are on page 32.

Glossary

alternating
(AWL-tur-*nayt*-ing)
changing back and
forth, such as between
two colors

checkerboard
(CHEK-ur-bord)
a design that shows
squares in two
alternating colors

fawn (FAWN) a young
deer

irregular pattern
(ih-REG-yuh-lur PAT-
urn) a pattern that has
one or more similar
parts unequal in size,
shape, or in the way
they are arranged

spiral (SPYE-ruhl)
winding or circling
around a center

Index

Read More

Cleary, Brian P.
*A–B–A–B–A: A Book of
Pattern Play.* Minneapolis,
MN: Millbrook (2010).

Harris, Trudy. *Pattern
Fish.* Brookfield, CT:
Millbrook (2000).

Learn More Online

To learn more about patterns in the park, visit
www.bearportpublishing.com/SeeingPatternsAllAround

About the Author

J. Clark Sawyer lives in Connecticut. She has
edited and written many books about history,
science, and nature for children.

Answers for Page 30:

1. D; 2. A; 3. C; 4. B